Just Screws Everything Up

OTHER FOR BETTER OR FOR WORSE® COLLECTIONS

Starting from Scratch
"There Goes My Baby!"
Things Are Looking Up ...
What, Me Pregnant?
If This Is a Lecture, How Long Will It Be?
Pushing 40
It's All Downhill From Here
Keep the Home Fries Burning
The Last Straw
Just One More Hug
"It Must Be Nice to Be Little"
Is This "One of Those Days," Daddy?
I've Got the One-More-Washload Blues ...

RETROSPECTIVES

Remembering Farley: A Tribute to the Life of Our Favorite Cartoon Dog
It's the Thought That Counts ... Fifteenth Anniversary Collection
For Better or For Worse: The 10th Anniversary Collection

A *For Better or For Worse*® Collection

Just Screws Everything Up

by Lynn Johnston

Andrews and McMeel
A Universal Press Syndicate Company
Kansas City

FOR BETTER OR FOR WORSE® is distributed internationally by Universal Press Syndicate.

ISBN: 0-8362-2128-1

Library of Congress Catalog Card Number: 96-84531

First Printing, July 1996
Second Printing, October 1996

9

12

Panel 1: WHAT ARE YOU WRITING? A STORY ABOUT GORDON'S GARAGE. IF IT'S ANY GOOD, MAYBE THEY'LL RUN IT IN THE LOCAL PAPER.

Panel 2: WHAT DO YOU THINK?

Panel 3: WELL, YOU'VE GOT A RUN-ON SENTENCE THERE, ELIMINATE THIS COMMA, AND BEGIN THIS SENTENCE WITH A PREPOSITION. CHANGE THIS TO A DIRECT QUOTATION, AND....

Panel 4: INSIDE EVERY READER LURKS AN EDITOR, WAITING TO GET OUT.

Panel 5: HI, DAD! HOW'S IT GOIN? FINE, I....

Panel 6: 'BYE, MOM! – I'M HEADING OUT! I'LL GRAB A BURGER DOWNTOWN. I'M MEETING RHETTA, AN' THEN I'M GOING TO WORK! UH...

Panel 7: SEE YAH! 'BYE!

Panel 8: AMAZING, ISN'T IT... FOR 19 YEARS, ALL THAT ENERGY LAY DORMANT.

Panel 9: ISN'T IT NICE TO HAVE OUR BOYS BACK FROM COLLEGE, ELLY! UH HUH!

Panel 10: BUT WE DON'T SEE MUCH OF MICHAEL. HE WORKS ALL NIGHT, SLEEPS DURING THE DAY – AND, THE REST OF THE TIME HE'S OUT WITH HIS FRIENDS!

Panel 11: WELL, AT LEAST YOU KNOW HE'S THERE, EL! AT LEAST YOU KNOW HE'S HOME! YEAH...

Panel 12: – THERE'S FOOD MISSING.

16

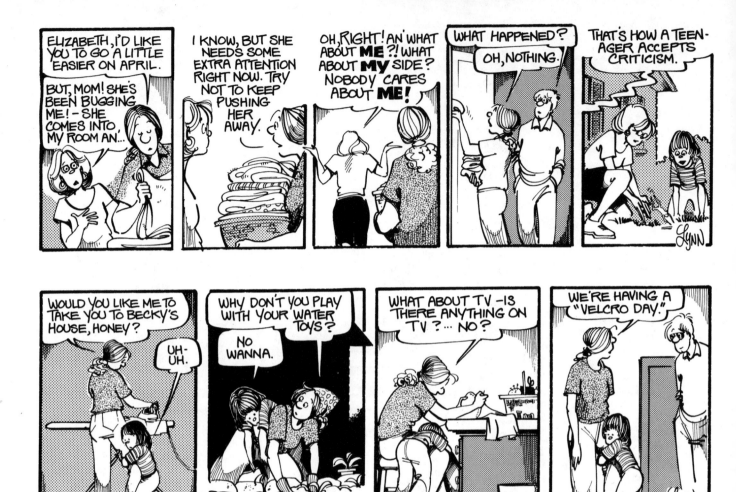

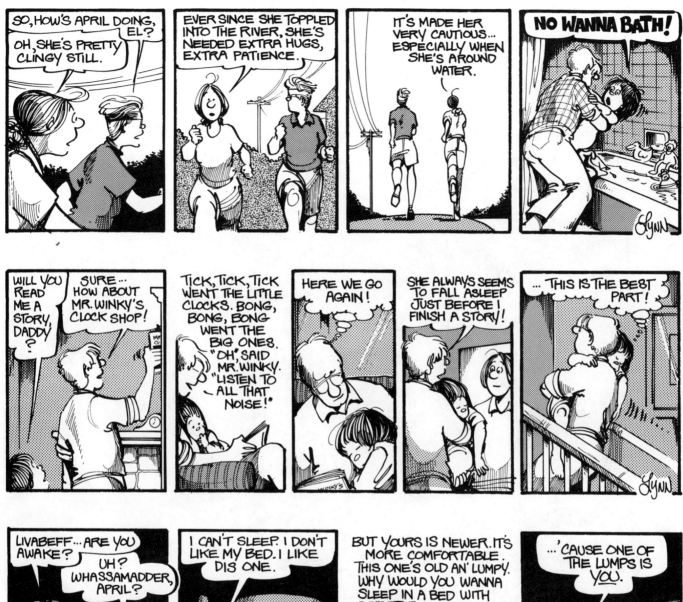

25

28

30

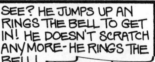

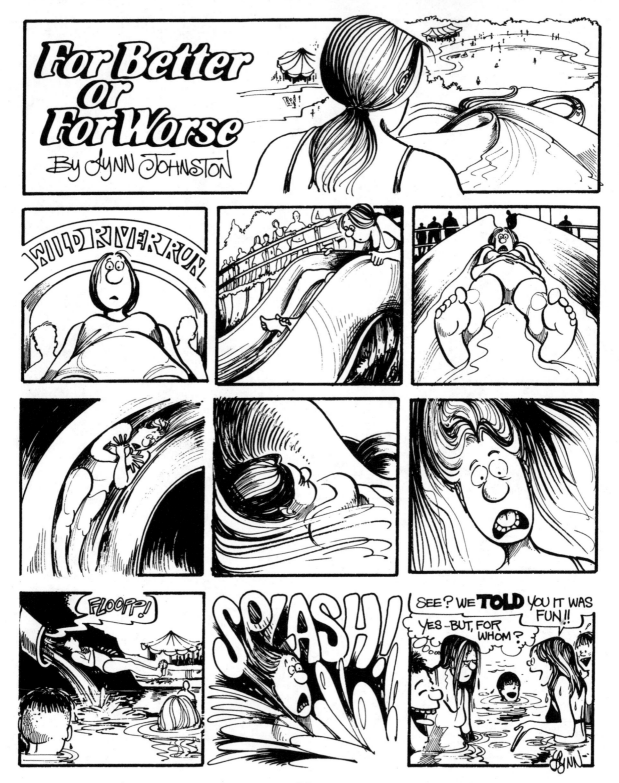

33

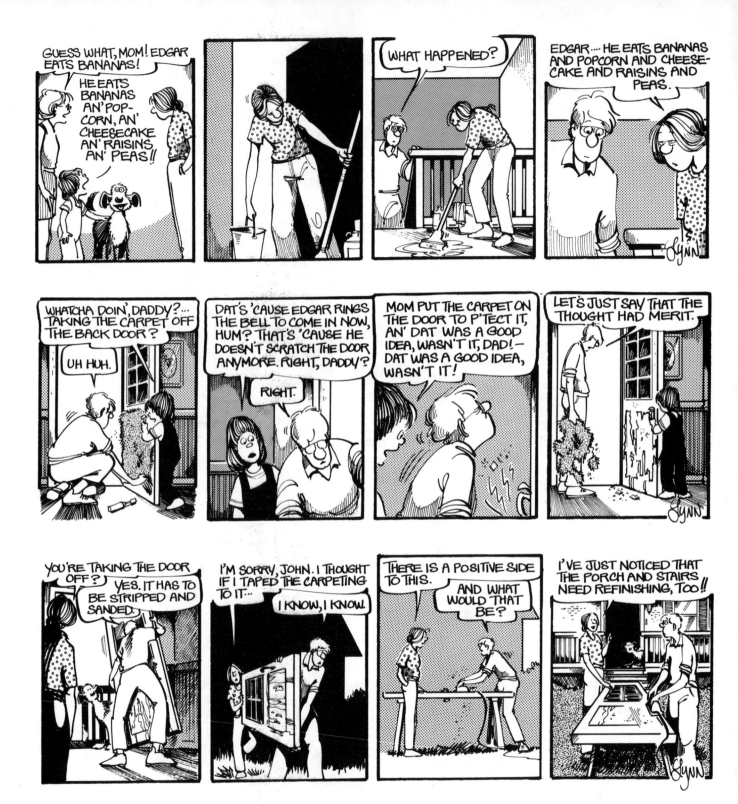

39

MOM, IF YOU'RE GONNA BE 45, HOW COME YOU ALWAYS SAY YOU'RE 39?

EVERYONE DOES THAT.... IT'S JUST SOMETHING PEOPLE DO.

BUT, ISN'T THAT A LIE?

NOT REALLY. WELL,... IT'S A LIE, BUT IT'S A "LITTLE WHITE LIE" WHICH MEANS IT'S NOT A **SERIOUS** KIND OF LIE.

BUT, IT **IS** A LIE, ISN'T IT? IF SOMEFING'S NOT THE TROOF, DEN IT'S A LIE! DAT'S WHAT YOU SAID! DON'T YOU ALWAYS HAFTA TELL THE **TROOF** IF SOMEONE ASKS YOU SOMEFING?

I DON'T KNOW, APRIL... THAT'S A "GREY AREA."

JOHN, CAN YOU TELL THAT I'M GOING GREY?

NOT REALLY.

LOOK. WHEN I PULL MY HAIR BACK LIKE THIS, YOU CAN SEE ALL THIS GREY!

OH. OK... NOW THAT YOU MENTION IT.

WHAT DO YOU THINK? SHOULD I COLOR MY HAIR, OR GO GREY NATURALLY?

I THINK YOU SHOULD LET NATURE TAKE ITS COURSE.

WHAT'S THAT SUPPOSED TO MEAN?

.... DO WHATEVER IT IS THAT'S IN YOUR NATURE!

OH, NO! YOU CAN'T **DO** THIS TO ME... **YOU PROMISED!**

SURPRISE!

WRINKLE CREAM, SENIOR'S VITAMINS, POLYDENT.... A CANE?

OVER THE HILL

AGING WITH GRACE

BUT THE BEST IS YET TO COME, EL!

WHAT'S THIS? ... A SPECIAL CLEANER FOR MY SPICE CONTAINERS?!!

...BECAUSE YOU CAN'T TURN BLACK THE CANS OF THYME!!!

43

WELL, WHAT DO YOU THINK? — IT'S A GOOD STORY, MICHAEL.

I KNOW.

BUT I'M NOT READY TO WRITE IT YET.

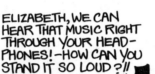

PROMISE ME YOU WILL SOMEDAY.

PROMISE ME. HERE, UNDER FARLEY'S TREE.

I PROMISE.

STRANGE... THERE ARE TIMES WHEN I THINK THAT TREE IS LISTENING.

BOOM CHA-KA BOOM CHA-KA BOOM, BOOM, BOOM CHA-KA

ELIZABETH, WE CAN HEAR THAT MUSIC RIGHT THROUGH YOUR HEADPHONES! — HOW CAN YOU STAND IT SO LOUD?!!

ELIZABETH? I SAID, WHY DO YOU HAVE THAT MUSIC TURNED UP SO DOGGONE **LOUD?!**

----------- ?
----------- !

LOOK AT THOSE FIELDS, KIDS! THAT'S REAL, HONEST-TO-GOODNESS PRAIRIE! THIS IS CANADA'S BREADBASKET. MUCH OF THE WORLD'S GRAIN COMES FROM HERE!

SEE THAT GRAIN ELEVATOR? THE FARMERS TRUCK THEIR GRAIN TO THE ELEVATOR WHERE IT'S ANALYZED, WEIGHED AND STORED FOR SHIPPING!

WHAT'S THAT OVER THERE, HONEY?

I DUNNO... LOOKS LIKE ONE OF THOSE THEME PARK WATER SLIDES.

REALLY?!! **WHERE?**

49

EVERYTHING ABOUT VANCOUVER IS SUCH A PART OF ME, DAD... THE PARKS, THE OCEAN, THE SMELL OF CEDAR AFTER A RAIN.

YOU MISS THE WEST COAST, DON'T YOU, ELLY.

I DO.

DO YOU EVER WISH YOU'D STAYED HERE?

NO, NOT REALLY.

WHY?

OH... I HAVE SEVERAL REASONS!

SO, ARE YOU NERVOUS, YET, GORDO?

I HAVEN'T HAD TIME TO BE NER-VOUS, GUYS!

I'M JUST GLAD THAT TRACEY DOESN'T MIND A SMALL WEDDING.

HEY, THAT'S NOTHING TO WORRY ABOUT!

YEAH.- MY GRANDMOTHER USED TO SAY THAT A WEDDING IS A BRIDGE THAT CONNECTS ONE SHORE TO ANOTHER...

BUT IT'S NOT THE SIZE THAT MAKES IT STRONG— IT'S THE NUTS THAT HOLD IT TOGETHER !!

THE WEDDING AND RECEPTION ARE GOING TO BE AT TRACEY'S PARENTS' HOUSE. THE FOOD IS ORGANIZED... IN FACT, I THINK EVERYTHING'S DONE!

WE HAVE SOME NICE GIFTS ALREADY, GUYS-AN' TRACEY'S FOLKS GAVE US A CHEQUE.

WHAT ARE YOUR FOLKS GIVING YOU, GORD?

I DUNNO -THERE'S ONLY ONE THING WE REALLY WANTED.

- WE ASKED THEM TO COME SOBER.

54

56

59

MAN, THE CAFETERIA IN THIS PLACE IS ABOUT TWICE THE SIZE OF OUR OTHER ONE!

AN' HAVING A CLASSROOM JUST FOR CHEMISTRY IS SO COOL!!

DON'T YOU LOVE ALL THE NEW STUFF, LIZ? — NEW SCHOOL, NEW COURSES, NEW TEACHERS...

— NEW GUYS!!!

DAWN, DON'T TURN AROUND, BUT THERE'S A GUY IN THE STAIRWELL WHO IS MAJORLY GORGEOUS!!

UH?

HOW CAN I SEE HIM IF I DON'T TURN AROUND?

PRETEND YOU'RE LOOKING IN THE TROPHY CASE, AN' LOOK THROUGH THE GLASS!

THE MOST IMPORTANT THING IS NOT TO LET THEM KNOW YOU'RE LOOKING!

OOOH! THE GRADE 11 AND 12 GUYS ARE SO AMAZING!!

YEAH!

WAIT A MINUTE, LIZ — AREN'T YOU STILL GOING OUT WITH ANTHONY?

YEAH, BUT I CAN LOOK, CAN'T I? I MEAN, IF HE CAN'T STAND A LITTLE COMPETITION...

KNOW WHAT TODAY WAS AT PRE-K, MOM? IT WAS "B" DAY! WE HAD TO DO EVERYTHING WIF "B"!

WE MADE BIRDS, WE PLAYED BALL, AN' WE HAD BUNS AT LUNCHTIME!

WOW!

LOOK, MOM! A "B"! DAT SIGN GOTS A "B" ON IT, RIGHT, MOM? IN FACT- IT GOTS TWO "B'S"! RIGHT, MOM?

I'M NOT SURE, APRIL...

TWO "B'S" OR NOT TWO "B'S" ... THAT IS THE QUESTION!!

... SOMETIMES I THINK MY MOM WORKS TOO HARD.

¡WHEW! WHAT A DAY!! — I HAD 3 EMERGENCIES, THEN AN ELECTRICAL PROBLEM BLEW OUT THE COMPUTERS AND SET OFF THE SMOKE ALARMS, SO WE HAD TO EVACUATE THE BUILDING.

KOMIX

I KNOW HOW YOU FEEL - WE WERE SHORTHANDED AT THE STORE, SO I GOT OFF WORK SO LATE I HAD TO GET APRIL FROM SCHOOL AND GO BACK INTO TOWN FOR GROCERIES! I AM BAGGED OUT!

FINE... I'LL MAKE SUPPER.

DON'T YOU JUST LOVE IT WHEN THEY VOLUNTEER?!!

SCRAPE SCRAPE SCRAPE

CLICK!

SCRAPE SCRAPE SCRAPE

CHOMP SMACK EAT CHOMP!

65

67

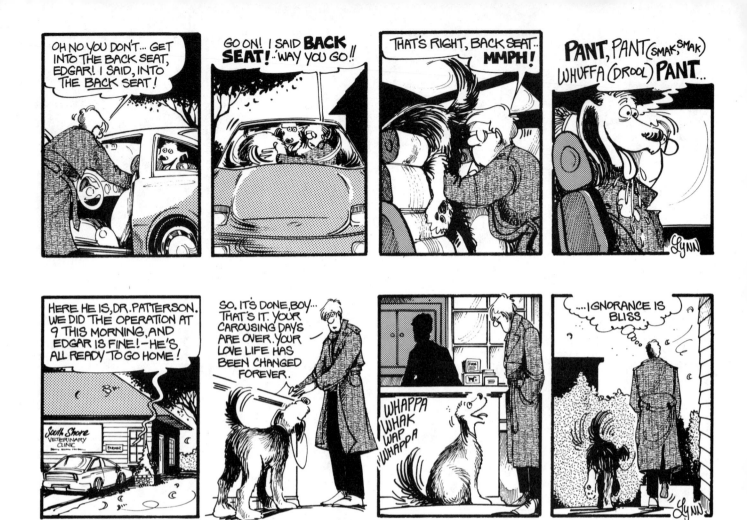

Panel 1: ELIZABETH, IT'S 8 O'CLOCK! WHY AREN'T YOU OUT OF BED?
UH?!!

Panel 2: I'VE GOT A SPARE FIRST THING. I DON'T HAFTA BE AT SCHOOL UNTIL 10!
BUT YOU STILL HAVE TO CATCH THE BUS!!

Panel 3: IT'S OK. ONE OF THE GRADE 12 GUYS IS PICKING ME UP.
YOU'RE GETTING A RIDE? WITH A BOY? IN A **CAR**?!!

Panel 4: TSK! WHAT'S SHE WORRIED ABOUT? I'M OLD ENOUGH TO TAKE CARE OF MYSELF!!!

Panel 5: ARE YOU KIDDING ME? YOU TWO GOT A RIDE WITH MATT LANDRY? ... HE'S GORGEOUS!!
TRUE.

Panel 6: HE'S A FRIEND OF MY BROTHER'S - AN' SINCE WE ALL HAD SPARES THIS MORNING, HE SAID HE'D PICK US UP!

Panel 7: I LOVE THIS SCHOOL. IT IS SO COOL TO BE AROUND OLDER GUYS FOR A CHANGE!
THERE'S JUST ONE PROBLEM, CANDACE.
WHAT?

Panel 8: ... WE'RE ALSO AROUND OLDER GIRLS!!

Panel 9:  NOW, YOU TELL ME. IS IT MY IMAGINATION, OR WAS THAT A SNEER?
IT WAS A SNEER.
IT WAS.

Panel 10:  WHAT IS IT WITH THE GRADE 11 AND 12 GIRLS, LIZ? THEY TREAT US LIKE ALIENS!

Panel 11:  WE'RE THE NEW KIDS ON THE BLOCK - FINE! BUT, ARE WE STUPID? ARE WE OUTCASTS? - WHAT ARE WE?!!

Panel 12:  ... COMPETITION.

Panel 1: I THINK YOU SHOULD GO AHEAD AN' DO IT, LIZ.

Panel 2: IN A NICE WAY, YOU HAVE TO TELL HIM YOU WANT TO GO OUT WITH SOMEONE ELSE!
RIGHT!

Panel 3: I MEAN, YOU'VE BEEN TALKING ABOUT BREAKING UP WITH ANTHONY FOR 2 OR 3 WEEKS NOW. SOONER OR LATER, HE'S GOTTA KNOW!!!
I KNOW.

Panel 4: ... AN' I'LL DO IT LATER.

Panel 5: THINK ABOUT IT, LIZ. THE LONGER YOU PUT OFF TELLING ANTHONY YOU WANNA BREAK UP WITH HIM - THE HARDER IT'S GONNA BE!!

Panel 6: LIKE, IF YOU DON'T WANNA TELL HIM, MAN - I WILL!!
REALLY?

Panel 7: WHY NOT? I COULD SAY THAT YOU LIKE HIM, AN' STILL WANT TO BE FRIENDS. YOU KNOW, THAT KINDA STUFF!
GEE, CANDACE...DO YOU THINK IT'S A GOOD IDEA?

Panel 8: HEY, WHEN YOU'RE GONNA DO SOMETHING LIKE THIS, IT'S IMPORTANT TO DO IT **RIGHT!**

Panel 9: WHAT'S HAPPENING, DAWN?
CANDACE IS OVER BY ANTHONY'S LOCKER, AN' THEY'RE TALKING.

Panel 10: THIS IS CRAZY. I'M THE ONE WHO WANTS TO BREAK UP WITH HIM!
NOT TO WORRY, LIZ...

Panel 11: —SHE'LL HANDLE IT OK.
DO YOU THINK SO?
SURE.

Panel 12: AFTER ALL...SHE'S DOING THIS FOR YOU!!!

79

85

91

97

98

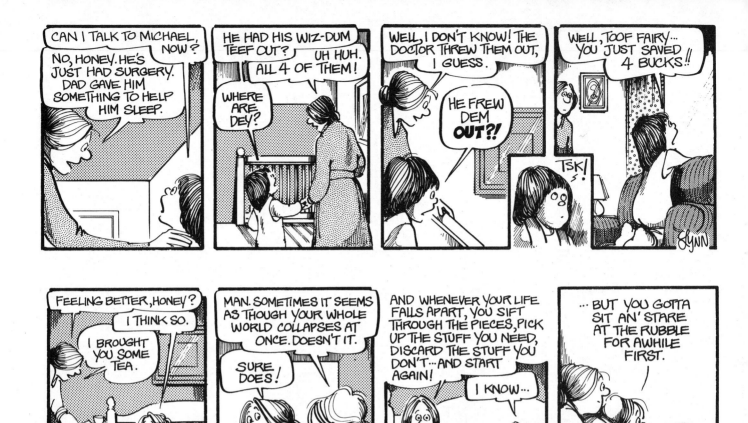

CAN I TALK TO MICHAEL, NOW?
NO, HONEY. HE'S JUST HAD SURGERY. DAD GAVE HIM SOMETHING TO HELP HIM SLEEP.

HE HAD HIS WIZ-DUM TEEF OUT?
UH HUH. ALL 4 OF THEM!
WHERE ARE DEY?

WELL, I DON'T KNOW! THE DOCTOR THREW THEM OUT, I GUESS.
HE FREW DEM OUT?!

WELL, TOOF FAIRY... YOU JUST SAVED 4 BUCKS!!
TSK!

FEELING BETTER, HONEY?
I THINK SO.
I BROUGHT YOU SOME TEA.

MAN. SOMETIMES IT SEEMS AS THOUGH YOUR WHOLE WORLD COLLAPSES AT ONCE. DOESN'T IT.
SURE DOES!

AND WHENEVER YOUR LIFE FALLS APART, YOU SIFT THROUGH THE PIECES, PICK UP THE STUFF YOU NEED, DISCARD THE STUFF YOU DON'T...AND START AGAIN!
I KNOW...

...BUT YOU GOTTA SIT AN' STARE AT THE RUBBLE FOR AWHILE FIRST.

WHAT AN EXCITING TIME THIS IS!

WITH ALL ITS RUSHING AND WRAPPING AND PLANNING AND COOKING AND VISITING AND LIGHTS AND SINGING AND CALLS AND LETTERS AND DECOR-ATIONS....

YES, SIR! THERE'S NOTHING LIKE CHRISTMAS!!

...AND I'M GLAD IT ONLY HAPPENS ONCE A YEAR!!!

MICHAEL, YOU AN' RHETTA ARE SUCH TOTALLY DIF-FERENT PEOPLE! — SHE'S GOING INTO BUSINESS WITH HER DAD — AN' YOU'RE A WRITER!

SHE PLANS TO STAY HERE THE REST OF HER LIFE — AND WHO KNOWS WHERE YOUR CAREER WILL TAKE YOU. MAYBE THIS BREAK-UP WAS FOR THE BEST.

THINK OF IT THIS WAY: YOU MET ON THE HIGH-WAY OF LIFE ... BUT YOU WERE TRAVELING IN DIFFERENT DIRECTIONS.

YEAH ...

I WAS A BUG — AND SHE WAS A WINDSHIELD!!

WELL, THIS PLACE IS LOOKING GOOD, GORDO. YOU TWO'VE SURE PUT IT TOGETHER

THANKS.

BUSINESS IS PICKING UP SINCE THEY WIDENED THE ROAD. WE'VE EVEN BEEN THINKING ABOUT PUTTING IN SOME EXTRA PUMPS.

TROUBLE IS, WE CAN NEVER GET AWAY! ONE OF US HAS TO BE HERE ALL THE TIME. WE'RE OPEN FROM 7 'TIL 10. SOMETIMES I WORK 'TIL 12, TRACEY DOES BOOKWORK ON THE WEEKEND ...

WE'RE MARRIED TO EACH OTHER, BUT WE'RE MARRIED TO THIS PLACE, TOO.

YEAH, NOBODY SAID LIFE WAS GONNA BE EASY, MAN. EVERYBODY'S GOT SOMETHIN' CHEWIN' AT 'EM!

ME, I TRY TO GET SOME-THIN' GOOD OUTTA EVERY DAY. KNOW WHAT I MEAN? LIKE, YOU FALL THROUGH THE SEAT IN THE OUT-HOUSE? WELL, AT LEAST IT'S A SOFT LANDING!

EVERY DAY HAS SOMETHIN' GOOD ABOUT 'ER. EVEN IF THAT SOMETHIN'S HARD TO FIND! — SO, THINK ABOUT 'ER, MIKE. WHAT'S GOOD ABOUT TODAY?!!

I'VE GOT YOU GUYS.

107

Panel 1: DAD, YOU'RE NOT ACTUALLY GOING OUT ON THE SKI HILL LIKE _THAT_, ARE YOU?

WHY NOT?

Panel 2: I'M WARM, I'M COMFORTABLE.

BUT NOTHING MATCHES!

Panel 3: ELIZABETH, THIS MAY COME AS A SHOCK TO YOU ... BUT I DON'T CARE!

Panel 4: .... SOME FOLKS LIKE TO BE SEEN, AN' OTHERS LIKE TO BE SKI-IN'!

Panel 5: WELL, DID YOU HAVE A GOOD TIME SKIING?

GREAT!

YAH!

Panel 6: WHAT HAPPENED?

I TOOK DOWN THE TREE AND PUT AWAY ALL THE CHRISTMAS DECORATIONS.

Panel 7: YOU MEAN, IT'S OVER?

UH HUH! EVERYONE'S BACK IN SCHOOL TO-MORROW—AND WE'RE INTO A BRAND-NEW YEAR.

WE ARE?!

Panel 8: ¡TSK¡ ... NOBODY TELLS ME _ANYFING_!

Panel 9: MICHAEL'S ONLY BEEN GONE FOR A FEW HOURS, BUT I MISS HIM ALREADY. WE SEE HIM SO SELDOM NOW.

Panel 10: ¡SIGH¡ I THINK ABOUT THOSE TEENAGE YEARS WHEN WE COULDN'T WAIT FOR HIM TO BE GONE ... AND ALL THAT STUFF SEEMS SO TRIVIAL NOW.

Panel 11: SLAM!

AAAGH! I HATE MY HAIR, I HATE MY GLASSES AN' I HATE THIS PLACE!!!

MY MOTHER IS WEIRD. ... TOTALLY ... WEIRD.

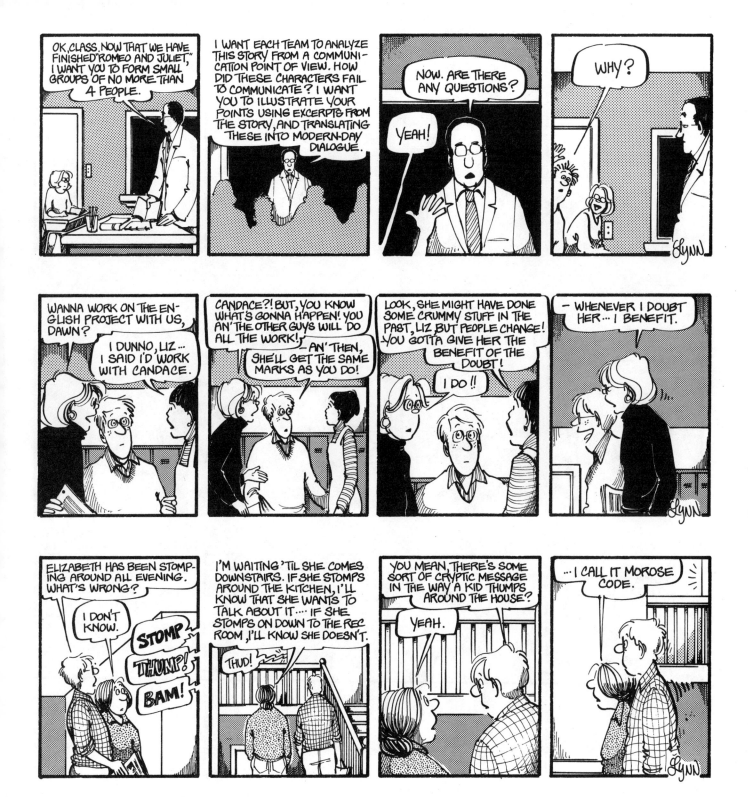

WHAT'S THE MATTER, LIZ? YOU'VE BEEN AWFULLY MOODY LATELY.

IT'S DAWN!!

SHE'S HANGING AROUND WITH CANDACE AGAIN... AN' I HATE CANDACE!

I THOUGHT YOU AND CANDACE WERE FRIENDS, TOO!

WE WERE.

BUT SHE'S ONLY YOUR FRIEND IF SHE WANTS SOMETHING!

AND WHAT DID CANDACE WANT FROM YOU?

TO BE FRIENDS WITH DAWN!!

YOU WANNA DO SOMETHING TOGETHER TONIGHT, DAWN?

UH...I'M GOING OVER TO CANDACE'S.

WANNA SEE A SHOW THIS WEEKEND?

MAYBE...IF CANDACE DOES.

MAN, I DON'T KNOW WHY YOU'RE HANGING AROUND WITH HER! YOU KNOW WHAT SHE'S LIKE! - SHE IS TOTALLY INSINCERE. SHE'S ONLY YOUR FRIEND IF SHE WANTS SOMETHING!

HOW CAN YOU SAY THAT, LIZ? I HAPPEN TO LIKE HER!!

BESIDES...I WANNA MEET HER OLDER BROTHER!

I HATE THIS LIFE, I HATE THIS PLACE. NOBODY CARES ABOUT ME....I HAVE NO FRIENDS!!!

NUDGE!

GO 'WAY, EDGAR.

I SAID, GO AWAY!!!

DOGS. THEY ALWAYS HAFTA COME AN' WRECK A PERFECTLY BAD MOOD!

I'M GOING DOWNTOWN, ELIZABETH. DO YOU WANT TO COME?

I DUNNO.

WELL, I'LL BE LEAVING IN 20 MINUTES. IF YOU'RE COMING, YOU'LL BE AT THE DOOR WITH YOUR COAT AND BOOTS ON.

BLEAH.

I HATE GOING PLACES WITH MY MOTHER. I'D RATHER BE WITH ANY-BODY BUT MY MOTHER! BEING SEEN WITH YOUR MOTHER MAKES YOU LOOK LIKE A TOTAL **WUSS**!!

I KNOW YOU'VE BEEN DE-PRESSED LATELY, LIZ. SOME-TIMES YOU JUST HAVE TO FORCE YOURSELF TO GET OUT AND DO THINGS!!

KNOW WHAT I DO WHEN I'M DEPRESSED? HAVE A CHANGE. I LOOK IN THE MIRROR AND I SAY TO MYSELF "IT'S TIME FOR A NEW ME!"

THEN, I FIND A WAY TO BE DIFFERENT! I CHANGE MY STYLE OF DRESS, I CHANGE MY MAKE UP, I CHANGE MY HAIR...

MAN! YOU HAVEN'T BEEN DEPRESSED FOR **AGES**, HAVE YOU, MOM!!

YOU KNOW WHAT I JUST REALIZED, MOM? YOU LOOK EXACTLY THE SAME AS YOU DID IN THE '60s!

WELL, EXCEPT FOR-YOU KNOW-WRINKLES AN' STUFF. BUT YOUR "LOOK" IS, LIKE, "PEACE AN' FLOWERS"... RIGHT?

BUT, HEY! THAT'S OK! YOU LOOK HOW YOU WANNA LOOK!

UH... ANY REASON YOU ASKED ME TO COME DOWNTOWN WITH YOU?

I WANTED TO CHEER YOU UP.

SO, I'M DRIVING DOWNTOWN WITH ELIZABETH, AND SHE TELLS ME I LOOK LIKE A LEFTOVER FROM THE '60s!

I'M TELLING YOU, CONNIE - IT'S BEEN ON MY MIND ALL WEEK!

ELIZABETH'S IN A FUNK, EL.

BY CRITICIZING YOU, SHE DUMPS SOME OF THE BLUES ON YOU, SEE?...IT SORT OF LIGHTENS THE LOAD!

...WELL...I JUST WISH HER WORDS DIDN'T WEIGH SO MUCH.

JOHN, DO YOU THINK I SHOULD CUT MY HAIR?

ELLY, THAT DECISION IS ENTIRELY UP TO YOU.

WHICH DO YOU LIKE BETTER... LONG HAIR OR SHORT?

I LIKE BOTH.

WOULD YOU LIKE ME WITH SHORT HAIR?

I'D LIKE YOU ANY WAY AT ALL!

SOMETIMES, ONE'S COMMITMENT TO MARRIAGE MEANS BEING NONCOMMITTAL.

COMB, BRUSH, PIN, BRUSH, COMB, PIN... AAAGH!

NO MATTER WHAT I DO, I STILL LOOK LIKE A FRUMPY, MIDDLE-AGED WOMAN.

I ASKED YOU A QUESTION!

124

Panel 1: WHAT'S WRONG? / MY RENT CHEQUE! I CAN'T FIND MY **RENT** CHEQUE!!

Panel 2: WHY DOES MY MOTHER SEND IT TO ME AN' NOT THE LANDLADY?!! SHE **KNOWS** I'M DISORGANIZED! SHE **KNOWS** I LOSE STUFF!!

Panel 3: ...DOES IT LOOK SOMETHING LIKE THIS?

Panel 4: YOU ALREADY ENDORSED IT, MAN... IT SAYS "PEANUT BUTTER, ROLL-ON, AN' CHEESE."

Panel 5: MAN, I CAN'T BELIEVE YOU USED YOUR RENT CHEQUE FOR A SHOPPING LIST!! / CAN IT, WEED.

Panel 6: YOU'VE BEEN TOTALLY FRIED LATELY, MIKE. YOU GOTTA GET OVER THIS RHETTA THING. / I'M OVER IT.

Panel 7: I'M SERIOUSLY OVER IT, OK? / WHOA! HE IS CHECKING OUT ANOTHER BABE!!

Panel 8: ... SHE LOOKED LIKE RHETTA.

Panel 9: IT'S VALENTINE'S DAY! I FORGOT IT WAS TODAY! / YOU DIDN'T FORGET, YOU SIMPLY REPRESSED IT.

Panel 10: BUT, HERE AT THE BUNG AND WATTLE, WE ARE GOING TO UNLEASH THOSE PENT-UP ANXIETIES, SEE .... AND FREE YOU FROM THE PAST!

Panel 11: COME ON, WEED, I CAN'T PARTY TONIGHT. WE'VE GOT AN EARLY CLASS TOMORROW. —YOU'LL HAVE TO WAKE ME UP, AN' CARRY ME THERE!!!

Panel 12: THAT, MIKE, IS WHAT FRIENDS ARE FOR.